A NO-NONSENSE, NO PHILOSOPHY, NO 1,000-PAGE MUMBO-JUMBO, PURELY PRACTICAL GUIDE TO NETWORKING FOR TODAY AND TOMORROW.

Jedidiah Irving Bressman

CONTENTS

PART 1: THE INTRODUCTION

If you picked up this practical guide, CON-GRATS. You are on your way to building life-long relationships and building your career. You may already know something about networking (or at least I hope you do), but this practical guide will help you refine your skills in a short-and-sweet manner.

Full Disclosure, I am not a Dr. of Networking (and yes, I do know that those do not exist, but it should). I am someone who struggled to maintain a well-balanced networking group. There are so many facets to efficiently and effectively network, and this practical guide will help keep it all straight. Correcting networking mistakes is no easy task. However, this practical guide will give you some handy skills needed to succeed where others have failed.

All the books I saw and read about networking felt more like a father scolding his child for bad behavior. (Heck, I attended a "financial seminar for millennials" where the financial advisor told us "millennials are hopeless." You can probably guess how much millennial business he got.) I did not feel a connection to those books. I felt like there was an element missing. That element, I believe, is a conversation between two people in the same stage of their life trying to make it through the complicated world of networking. That is what I want to give you in this practical guide. Networking is not easy. I repeat networking is not easy. But, done effectively, networking can enhance your life both personally and professionally.

Networking is both an art and a skill. But to understand the intricacy of networking, you need to understand the concepts of how to efficiently and effectively network. If you take one thing away from this practical guide, and one thing only, it should be this:

Networking should be about relationship building and the exchange of information, not job hunting or sales building.

When you base your networking relationship on job-hunting and sales-building, you miss out on the opportunity of building trust with your networking partner. You should be networking for the right reasons, not for some ulterior motive. Without trust, you will be unable to land the job or the sale intended. This is not to say that *eventually,* this relationship could help you build leads or land you a job, but that is not the point of networking. The point of networking is to build a group of friends who work for the benefit of each other.

Networking is like a passive investment; it works for you and works even when you are not looking. Unfortunately, though, networking is changing, and people think millennials cannot meet someone, professionally, and not be asked the ultimate question, "Can you get me a job?" I say they are liars and generalists. Millennials are ruining everything right? Does that include networking? I think not. We just need some fine-tuning. That is what this practical guide will help you do.

The "Can you get me a job" question is the ultimate relationship building killer, and as you read through this practical guide, you will learn how to network. More on this later. Too many people tell me that they are surprised that I did not ask them for a job the first time we meet. The job-hunting mindset is a networking and relationship killer. Why would you want to meet with someone or be with someone that has a one-sided mindset? If you think this way, you need to change your mindset. This practical guide will help you learn that networking can lead to a job, but this should not be the expectation.

Before we begin, let's walk through the start

of the networking relationship. You will find this relationship starts well before the first meeting. The best way to begin a connection is organically. Meeting a person through a mutual interest and then connecting with them on a professional level cuts out the awkward "first date." However, there are plenty of other ways how to begin a connection. This practical guide will touch on ways to find those connections that will benefit you. I will illustrate to you how to research your future networking partner.

Second, I will help you with what I call the "first date." While networking and dating are very different, you will find that there are plenty of similarities. What you should wear, what you should talk about, will they like you, are all examples of questions you will ask yourself before you meet with your networking partner. Sound familiar? I will take you through a step-by-step way to connect with the person. These steps include (1) topics of conversation; (2) what questions to ask; (3) what to order; (4) where to meet; and finally, (5) how to set up the next meeting. There are multiple other items to consider when going on the "first date," but you will have to keep reading to get those.

Finally, I will discuss the maintaining and strengthening of this relationship. Remember, a personal relationship and a professional relationship are two very different relationships, but you may not be able to tell which connection you are building with the person. I will discuss the two groups of networking connections that you will meet and what you should do with each group. Finally, we will discuss how you can benefit from the relationship.

Mastering these four segments of networking, you will gain the tools to efficiently and effectively network. I hope you enjoy this Practical Guide. Happy Networking!

PART 2: WHAT IS THE POINT OF NETWORKING?

This is a practical guide, so I will not bore you too much with the "philosophy" of networking, but if someone gifted you this practical guide by a family or friend, you might be thinking "Why should I network?" Or even "What is the point of networking? I already have enough friends."

Remember in middle school when you had your "clique?" Think of your networking group as your clique. These are the people who will be by your side for the ups and downs of your personal life and professional career. These people will be friends, business colleagues, former bosses, or even someone in a completely different sector, but all your network should have one goal in mind, "How can we mutually benefit each other?" When I network with someone for the first time, I want to focus on what can I do for them. If I focus on what I could do for them, you will lose the "me first" mentality that plagues a networking relationship from the start. Everyone has something positive to offer.

How can we mutually benefit each other?

I have a networking relationship with Millennials, Gen-Xers, Baby Boomers, and people in between. No person is too old or too young to be in your networking group. Each person has something to offer depending on what you are looking for.

Most people start networking too late to effectively leverage their network. People use networking as a tool to get a job. While networking could, eventually, lead to job opportunities, people miss the point of truly connecting with people if they only view it as a tool to get a job. So, if you are starting from scratch, you have your work cut out for you.

Think of your network as a passive investment. When you invest in other people and build those relationships, those people are willing to invest in you. Your network works for you, and most of the time, it works for you when you are not looking. You know the saying, "A watched pot never boils?" Well, your network does not always work when you are watching.

Let me give you an example, after working as an attorney in a government office for eighteen months, my roommate told me about a job opportunity in a different government agency. I tried to look online for the position but could not find it posted anywhere. How did I get this unposted position? A few of my connections (in-person, not LinkedIn) told me about the position. Those people thought I should apply. So, I did. What I did not know, at the time, was how my network was helping me.

Two of my connections sent my resume directly to my current boss. Multiple others talked to him at casual events. All these people helping me. People I met through networking and building a relationship with them. My networked worked for me and I did not know it until sometime after I got the position. Sometimes, your network is helping you without you having to ask, just like a passive investment. But, unlike a passive investment, your network helps you build a career.

Look, having the skills to succeed in your job is always the first step. I will never suggest that you can get a job (or a network that works for you) without having the proper qualifications. While who you know might get you the job, if you do not have the skills to succeed at the job, your network cannot help you. Every person who recommends you is putting their reputation on the line. Think about this as a friend recommending a new restaurant in town. If you go to their recommendation and it is a nightmare are you likely to ask that friend for another restaurant suggestion? Probably not.

Remember, your network is a push and pull. You help them, they help you. But when you help each other you are telling your network to support this person. If you do not have the skill to succeed, people are less likely to vouch for you (since their credibility is on the line).

Let me give you one more example. While I worked for my first government agency, I saw a position open. I looked through the description and thought that I would like to be in that position. I went online and found a person who formerly held that position. I emailed him and asked if he would like to have lunch and tell me about his time working in that position. He agreed. We had an amazing conversation and by the end of this meeting, he had convinced me that I would not like that position. What did I get from the meeting? We found a way to work together on a project that mutually benefitted us. From that meeting, I gained a lifelong friend.

Alright, the pep talk over. Let us get into the meat and potatoes. How does one figure out who to network with?

PART 3:
RESEARCHING

One of the most essential steps of networking is knowing the person you are meeting. While you might know their profession, their college, or their general personality you may not know anything more than that. Researching the person or the company they work is the first key in developing a relationship.

For example, if you Google me, you will see the information you probably already know. No really, go to Google and put in my name. What do you see? What did you learn? You probably learned that I am a lawyer (or you knew that from reading this practical guide). What else did you find? That I used to wrestle? That I used to be a radio DJ? Did you see my LinkedIn profile? This is a great way to start your research. A simple Google search and you now have multiple topics of conversation. Multiple ways to connect with your networking partner.

Another way to research and build your network is to become affiliated with a non-profit group that you care about. Research those non-profits in your area that you align with. In law school, I worked as a legal fellow for a local non-profit that I care deeply about, and I enjoyed what the non-profit did for my community. As a legal extern, I worked with their finance people to redevelop their college grant program for local students. I spent hours working with a great group of people. By the time I finished my externship, I became good friends with the CEO. He and I still meet for coffee once a month. Now I sit as a fellow on their investment committee. All these connections made by doing something I am passionate about.

Each new activity you do is a networking opportunity, but only if you make it one. When I talk about networking with my peers, it seems to be a foreign concept. However, if you try to network by doing the activities you love, you will meet many new and interesting people with common interests and connections. Putting in the time by researching each new opportunity will not guarantee that it will be successful, but if you do not research, your chances of a successful network are slim.

Most people love to do one thing, talk about themselves. There is no better way to get your networking partner to talk about themselves than to bring up a hobby or a former sport. You are building a connection with this person. I will repeat this often in this practical guide, networking is like dating. There might be specific information you would want to know ahead of time. You might want to know their job, favorite food, hobbies, etc. Do not go overboard, though. That is an easy way to offend your networking partner.

Why is this even important? First, you want to make sure you understand who they are as a person. Some people will judge you from the first handshake, whether they can have a beer with you, or if you just seem like a good person. Again, networking is like dating. You want to make sure you understand where they are coming from. Especially, if they are from a different culture. You do not want to offend them.

Also, do not forget that the reason you are networking with people is to learn more about the person. Learn their story. How did that person get where they are? Ask questions about their history. If you focus the entire conversation on yourself and your goals, you are missing a valuable opportunity to connect with that person. Researching the person helps you build this connection and know the questions (and usually the answers) before you meet with them.

Imagine having no connections, in a world full of people. How do you begin to network?

You could always start by blindly emailing someone you are interested in meeting, but this will not be the most effective route. (However, as I showed above, it can work). One of the best ways to network is through friendship. Being able to say "Hi, I'm _____ and your friend ____ said we would get along. Let us grab coffee soon," is a great way to begin relationship building. Just meet with a lot of people "cold-calling" them for coffee.

If you went to college, I recommend reaching out to your career services team to see about alumni in your area of interest. If you did not go to college, ask your parents or a friend if they know anyone in your area of interest. Having an initial connection with something can significantly boost the likelihood of having a successful networking experience.

I like being the person who can recommend to other people. My undergrad friends ask me for lawyer referrals for various projects that they are working on. I like being able to connect them and help them reach their goals. But I also like helping my friends network with people to get to their goals.

For example, a lawyer friend of mine had been interested in clerking for a judge. When an unposted position became open at the court, I went to the judge and asked her if I could send her the application of my friend. The judge graciously agreed. While my friend ended up not being chosen for the position, she did get offered the job to clerk for another judge. This made me happy to see my friend be able to do a position that she wanted to do. Even if the position came in a roundabout way.

Let us assume you had a family member give you an idea for who to network with. Where do you start? Here are the steps you should follow in researching your networking partner:

Step 1. Start with a Google search.

What did you find? Click on a few of the links and read through them. When you discovered a common interest, you have a topic of conversation. I find a mutual interest in a subject will get the first networking off to a great start. I suggest finding two-three subjects to ask them about. The conversation should flow smoothly and organically. Even though you should come prepared, do not force a conversation. because if you have met the right person, they will be interested in you too. ALWAYS BE PREPARED.

Step 2. Is your connection on LinkedIn?

I use LinkedIn more than I use Facebook. You should be using LinkedIn for your networking connections because it is built as a business profile. You will learn about their past. What organizations are they affiliated with? You can read their posts and even see if you have any mutual connections with them. You will see their education, mutual connections, and past jobs.

Step 3. Check out their Bio.

Looking through their company bio will also have some tidbits of information. You will learn about their accomplishment and skills. Maybe you will learn they have two kids and one of them plays your favorite sport. Sharing an alma-mater is another great way to become a personal connection.

Step 4. Ask Around.

Utilize your current network. Does anyone in your network know the person you are going to network with? Not only will this help you build that initial connection with the person, but you will learn more about them as a person. Your friend can tell you what gets your future networking connection excited and what makes them tick.

These four steps will ensure you are prepared to meet with your networking connection. Understanding the person, who they are, what they do, and how they do it will help guide you to a successful mentoring relationship. Hopefully, one that builds and leads to a better future.

Now that you have done your research, you are ready for the "First Date."

PART 4: THE "FIRST DATE"

I have referenced this before, but in case you skipped a Part (like I have been known to do when I was in law school), networking is like dating. You might find yourself awkwardly tugging at your food or coffee, or even sitting through a few awkward silences. If you have done your research, then you will have nothing to worry about. However, let us tackle some of the stuff you should also be thinking about.

Step 1.   What Will You Wear?

Let us start with the before. You need to dress for the occasion. I am a firm believer that you will never be overdressed with a suit and tie or some other professional outfit. But you also need to be comfortable. If you are meeting with a business professional for the first time, wear a professional outfit. If you are meeting with someone who's job does not require professional dress, then wear jeans and polo. You need to dress comfortably, but you also want to make a good first impression.

Like I said before, I would always wear a suit and tie. Not only do I think it is professional, I think it makes a statement that I care. My father is a lawyer too, but you might never guess it by the way he dresses. He hates wearing a suit and tie. (A lawyer who hates a suit and tie, who knew?) Ultimately, he does not wear a suit and tie to work is because he believes that he can connect with his client. As a personal injury lawyer, you are normally not representing the millionaires. A personal injury lawyer is representing those are down on their luck because of an accident. He finds his clients and potential clients are more receptive to someone who is like them rather than "looking up" at a fancy dressed lawyer. I tell you this story not so you can "dress down," but so that you will think about what you are going to wear and how your networking partner might receive your outfit.

Step 2.   When Will You Arrive?

Out of all the mishaps that could take place, you can only control a select few. One of them is what time you will arrive. Being early is a sign of respect. Plain and simple. You are communicating with your connection that you value their time. But, it also allows you to get comfortable with your landscape. If your networking connection is late, do not be upset or show your frustration with their lateness (even though you might want to).

For example, if your connection has indicated they want to meet at a coffee shop you have never been to, you will want to make sure you go to the right one. Then you will want to get your coffee and take a seat at a table. By arriving early, you can get comfortable in your space. Networking is already difficult enough, especially when you are meeting someone new. Being comfortable with one aspect of the meeting goes a long way.

Always arrive 5-10 minutes early.

Step 3.   What do I say?

You have picked your outfit, you have arrived early, and you are ready to go. Now to the hard part. I am going to give you some "Do's" and Do Nots to help guide you.

    a. DO introduce yourself.
    b. DO NOT read them your bio.
    c. DO ask them questions about them.
    d. DO NOT interrupt them.
    e. DO listen to what they have to say.
    f. DO NOT try and "one-up" them with your own story.

True story. A few of my friends recommended I network with a lawyer, who ended up becoming a deputy director of legal, in another government agency. I set it up, did my research, and met him at a coffee shop. The first thing he said to me? "Look, I just want to be upfront, I cannot get you a job in my office. I do not have any hiring power." I sat there puzzled. I just wanted to meet with someone who my other connections thought I should meet. After explaining that I was not asking him for a job, I asked him why he would lead off with that. His answer shocked me. "I meet with a lot of people your age. They start the conversation with an ask for a job. I just got tired of it." Can you blame him?

The general steps for "first date" success include (1) topics of conversation; (2) what questions to ask; (3) what to order; (4) where to meet; and finally (5) how to set up the next meeting. Again, it sounds like a date, right? You should have the first two steps down from reading Chapter 1: Researching.

One final note. Try to avoid talking about politics, religion, or money. Except, of course, if you know they are likely to agree with you or they enjoy debating those topics. These topics are touchy subjects and are more likely to make them (or you) upset rather than building a relationship.

Step 4.   Where Should You Meet?

Why are we talking about this? Because you would be surprised at the places some people ask to meet. Choose a place that is not loud. Some coffee shops are better than others. You cannot connect with someone you cannot hear. Scope out a few places you think you might want to meet your networking connections. Of course, if your networking partner suggests a place, look it up first before agreeing. If you are not comfortable going to a side of town, or if you know that you will be uncomfortable, speak up. If your networking connection gets upset that you deny their first choice, then they probably are not someone you want to connect in the first place.

Step 5. How Should You Set Up The Next Meeting?

Look, you have a busy schedule and so do they. Be proactive in setting up the next meeting. Do not rush it though. Send a follow-up email (or even better a handwritten card) thanking them for meeting with you. Then in a few weeks, follow-up again, but this time with a reason to meet. You show initiative, but you also show interest.

Reflect on these five steps. Think about how you can implement them into your next networking meeting. Now that you have finished the "First Date," let us finish up on the hardest part of networking.

PART 5: BUILDING AND MAINTAINING YOUR NETWORKING RELATIONSHIP

I want to take the next few pages to finish up this practical guide by talking about continuing your networking relationship. You have done the easy part (believe it or not). Now you must maintain the relationship. You have completed the "First Date." Great job. You may not realize it now, but you have begun a potentially life-long connection. An equally important aspect of networking is maintenance. But again, like dating, if you liked the "first date," you cannot just stop talking to the person and expect to hear from them or benefiting from the relationship. The maintaining part of the networking relationship may ultimately be the hardest, but also the most fulfilling part of the relationship.

First, determine what type of relationship you want with your networking partner. Is the person someone you want to network with regularly? This person falls into the core network group. Is the person someone who you would like to continue connecting with, but not all the time? There are two groups of networking connections that you will have.

1. **Your "Core" Group. (5-7 People).**
2. **Your Casual Circle (Unlimited).**

Your "core" group should be the people whose opinions matter most. In politics, politicians call this their "Kitchen Cabinet." A "Kitchen Cabinet" has all the essentials and so does your "core" group. These should be your biggest supporters, your toughest critics, and your fiercest allies. When looking for professional advice, this should be the group you call first to get their advice. Parents are great at general life advice (unless your father/mother shares the same profession that you do. Then they can give you professional advice), but your "core" group helps you think about the subjects that your family may not be able to bring out.

I tend to meet with my core network group, individually, about once a month or every six months (depending on their availability). I limit my core network group to around 5-7 people. That does not mean every meeting is a "networking" event. Sometimes my wife and I go on double dates with my connections. Although, they inevitably like my wife more than me, and who can blame them?

Be careful of having too many in your core network group. If you do, you will not be able to build a one-on-one relationship with each one. Again, networking is about relationship building. Those 5-7 people will take that many hours per month for your networking partners. While that may not seem like a lot of time, you must think about work, personal life, and even new connections. Your exterior network will still take up some time and so will your new relationships. I tend to have one "new" networking meeting per week along with one core network meeting.

During these meetings, we catch up on life, how each other is doing, what we are excited about coming up in the next month, how work is going. But we also discuss opportunities. In what way can I benefit you? And vice-versa? What better way to build a relationship than to work together for a common goal or even to help your mentor or mentee in achieving their goal? Always be thinking of ways you can benefit your networking partner. Thinking selflessly will always gain you points. I cannot stress enough, networking is not about a job, it is about relationship building.

Your casual circle includes people you meet with occasionally. Again, your "core" group and will be working like passive investments. Giving you people to network with and advocating people on your behalf. But, every networking meeting, just like dating, will not go as planned. This group of people can still be advocates for you and visa-versa, but these are not people you try to network with every month or every six months. It is a hard choice of who to have in each category, and your core group will be fluid, but keeping these circles will help you differentiate who you should be meeting regularly.

When networking meetings fail to meet expectations, I would never burn the bridge. Do not burn any bridge in your networking life, especially if you are networking within your field. You do not know who the person is and who that person knows, and you do not want someone giving you a bad rap. I have spent time mending bridges that I burned by being immature and not understanding the value of networking.

BONUS PART: NETWORKING IN THE AGE OF COVID-19

This practical guide has taken many forms of the time I have sat down to write it. However, over the past month as I have been in quarantine has made me think of one more part this book needs. A discussion about networking in COVID-19.

I have always been someone who prefers in-person meetings. There is just something about meeting someone in person that makes me feel better about the networking relationship I am building. However, COVID-19 does not allow for that, so how can you continue to network.

Let us start with you Core Group that we

discussed in Part 5. Call them and check in on them. They are in the same boat as you are. How can you help them get through this difficult time? My Wife and I delivered cinnamon rolls to some of our friends. No contact, just cinnamon roll delivery. Who can beat that?

I think you will be surprised at how appreciative people are that you care. Some people are going through more difficult times than others. Some of your friends, co-workers, and network may have had a family member who had COVID-19 or lost a job. Check in on them. Focus on your connection with them. If they need help, help them. Stop thinking about the "What will this do for me?" or even worse "How can this person help me?" Rather, you should be focusing on how you can truly help someone in their time of need.

If you are still determined to network, and I hope you are, look into meeting someone by zoom or by phone. Do not stop reaching out to people just because you are stuck at home. This is the best time to continue building your network if you can. If not? Do not worry. There will be plenty of time to build your network when you are healthy and not social distancing.

CONCLUSION

L ook, this is a practical guide. I could go on for another 150 pages telling you about every detail about networking, but you are reading this practical guide because you need the "quick and dirty." This guide is your first step into creating a new future for yourself. The power of networking will work wonders for you and is a great tool in your arsenal. Use it wisely.

You should reach out to me if you would like to connect. I want to know how we can help each other. You can connect with me by email at JedidiahBressman@gmail.com. You can listen to my podcasts at https://networkingcoach.podbean.com/

ACKNOWLEDGEMENT

Thank you to my network who read, revised, and helped me through this process. I am incredibly excited to have you all as my friends and I cannot wait to continue building our relationship.

ABOUT THE AUTHOR

Jedidiah Irving Bressman

Jedidiah is an attorney in Ohio. When he is not practicing law or workng on building relationships, Jedidiah is spending time with cooking, puzzling, or traveling with his wife. You can connect with him on Linkedin at www.linkedin.com/in/jedid-iahbressman,